I Heard a
CHRISTMAS
Whisper

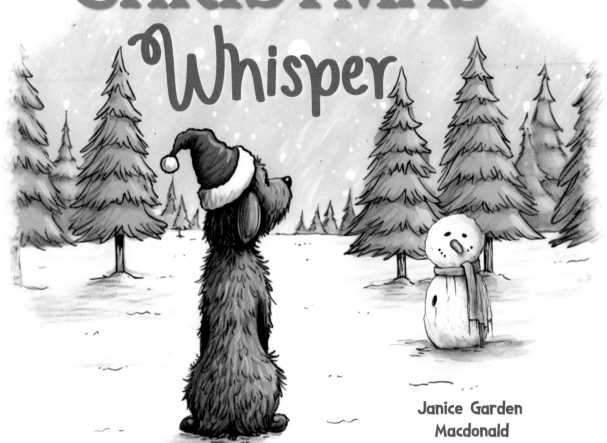

Janice Garden
Macdonald

Back Pack Books

ISBN: 9798864890875

All rights reserved 2023

BACK PACK BOOKS
Ontario, Canada
Backpackbooks.ca

I Heard Christmas Whisper
by
Janice Garden Macdonald

This book is dedicated to
the famous
Sycamore Gap Tree
(Robin Hood Tree)
circa 1700- 2023

MERRY CHRISTMAS EVERYONE!a

I heard Christmas whisper

It's quiet like snow

I saw Christmas shining

All twinkle and glow

I felt Christmas coming

It came from above

It smelled like a forest

And felt like love

It followed me home

And Christmas grew

And **grew**

And **grew**

And then one day

It just couldn't stay

Sometimes I miss Christmas

It's soft like snow

It stays for a while

But then it must go

Can you hear Christmas whisper?

It's always close by

It comes back each year

And whispers a sigh

I still think about Christmas

But I never feel blue

Christmas lives in my heart, now

It can live in yours too!

The End

Love to Read, Love to Learn

More by this author

Do Butterflies Sleep?
Do Ants Have Uncles?
Do Beetles Sing?
Do Bees Say Please?
Do Flies Tell Lies?

BackPackBooks.ca

SCAN FOR MORE GREAT BOOKS
& Resources
Stories kids love, themes parents love

BackPackBooks.ca

14834364R00021